THE DOUGH

TECHNICAL ASPECTS

History says that in 1889, while King Humbert I and his wife Margaret were spending the summer in Capodimonte above Naples, they tasted a local dish which they had heard a lot about.

This was how Don Raffaele and his wife Rosa, owners of the most famous pizzeria in Naples, made their entrance into the King's kitchens where they prepared three pizzas. Everyone knows the Queen preferred the one made with tomatoes, mozzarella and basil which has used her name, Margherita, ever since.

Loyal to their secrets Rosa and Don Raffaele passed on nothing, except some news about what had happened. One sure thing is that the pizza they made would not be possible nowadays. Too many things have changed since then. The famous Naples water, which those wily Neapolitans have always told us is the secret ingredient of the best pizzas in the world, has disappeared down some underground cavern or is being piped directly into the Mediterranean. The mills which ground the flour have been taken over by giant factories or by warehouses where they import grain from the four corners of the world. The tomato paste is prepared under the same sun, but the plant itself has changed, and the buffaloes (or the cows) still make mozzarella, but they are fed something else.

However, all is not lost. Industry on the one hand, and good professionals on the other, still offer new products and new solutions which can be enjoyed today.

Even so, now as then, one cannot ignore the basic ingredients: flour, water, salt, and yeast and sometimes oil, all of which we're going to look at closely.

Flour

The fundamental ingredient.

To discuss all the types and varieties of flour would be beyond the scope of these pages, so we shall only look at a few essential characteristics.

The term "flour" means a product obtained by milling wheat. The characteristics of the flour depend upon the type of wheat, where it was grown, and how exactly it is ground. Flour is mainly divided into two categories, durum wheat and soft grain. Flour made from durum wheat is used to make pasta (durum means "hard" in Latin) but it's not so widespread in the bread-making process even if in southern Italy it is added to soft grain to make some exquisite local breads.

Soft grain is whiter in colour, and flour made from this type is more widely used. In Italy it is usually ground to either "0" size, which is slightly coarse, or "00", giving a much finer texture or finesse. The finer "00" flour is used more often especially in pizzerias. In this book we will refer to "flour milled to 0 and 00 finesse" quite often even though, outside Italy, this may be a value of little or no importance. The reason is that the pizza maker that gave that particular recipe stressed its importance.

The most important factor to consider when choosing the flour for pizza is its *strength*, which is indicative of the volume that the mixture can take. This is measured in "W" units, where a high W means "strong " flour and a low W "weak" flour. A good pizza flour should have a W no lower than 260-280 (even if the disciplinary of the *Associazione Verace Pizza Napoletana* says the W has to be somewhere between 220 and 380). A lower value can be used, but the dough will not be so good and there may be other drawbacks especially if you aren't a professional and don't know how to manage everything properly. If the strength of the flour isn't shown on the packet, ask your supplier or contact the company directly to find out.

There are countless types of flour on the market. Pizza makers usually have a fairly wide choice when buying.

One of these choices is to contact the flour manufacture direct, those that specialise in making and studying high quality flour specifically for pizza. I am not trying to do anything underhand, but it is a matter of fact all professionals recognise. Nobody uses a packet of flour they've bought from the corner shop, because it almost certainly won't be very good for professional use (since it most likely will not be a strong flour). Very few pizza-makers are capable of fixing specific faults in a batch of flour to get a well balanced final product. Lots of companies guarantee constant quality standards and often they offer their clients assistance and advice as to which flour is best for their particular needs. They can even make a special mix, although clearly this will cost a bit more. Don't worry that your pizza will be exactly like all the others: small variations such as the temperature in your work room, water, oil, and different yeast, or also the simple way you knead the dough will have an effect on the final result, making it unique.

Otherwise, you can turn to any number of local manufacturers and ask them to try and meet your needs, or another option is to try and mix various flours yourself. At the end of the day special flour for pizzas is only a mix of quality milled wheat, which someone else has already mixed for you and you can just as easily do the same thing. You can be creative or even have a go at a bit of alchemy: this takes time but if you get it right you could end up with a spectacular flour mix.

Almost all recipes are for this type of procedure, not because it is the most widespread practice, or the one that automatically gives the best results, but it offers you a choice and you can try out many different ways before you settle for the one you like best.

It is always a good rule to let your flour settle for a couple of weeks before you start making dough with it; even in small restaurants, it is best to keep flour in special, raised hoppers to keep it away from humidity.

Water

Water is the other vital ingredient of pizzas. It must be drinking water, and it must not have any strange taste or smell. It must be of medium hardness, i.e. somewhere between 5 and 20 dGH (degrees of General Hardness) even if some professionals hold the best range is between 12 and 18 dGH.

The acidity of the water, its pH, is important too, and the best range is somewhere between 5 and 7 as it affects the final pH of the dough. When the water is too hard, it is difficult for carbon dioxide to form, and your dough will not rise so easily or it will take longer and it will be less elastic. The opposite is when the water is too soft, the dough can be sticky and almost rubbery. If something seems to be wrong with your dough, you can use a piece of indicator paper to test the acidity of the water. Sometimes hardness is just temporary and to lower the pH you need only to boil it for a few minutes, add a little vinegar even if it may affect the final taste, or use some bottled water. If the water is too soft put salt in with the water and add the yeast halfway through the dough-making process.

Tradition says that your water must sit at room temperature for a couple of hours before you use it, the so called *acqua ferma*. Truth be told many of us use tepid water to speed up rising, or slightly chilled to slow it down, but you must be aware of what you are doing. When the water is too cold, especially in winter, the rising can slow down so much that the dough becomes hard and once cooked it will be flat and rigid. Otherwise, if the water is too warm, the dough can rise too quickly and lose all its elasticity. We shall look at this subject again when we deal with yeast.

You can use mineral water, and if you are brave enough you can even use sparkling water to make your dough crispier.

The average amount of water needed for the dough is somewhere between 50 and 65% of the weight of the flour: strong and high quality flour needs less water. The type of yeast you use also affects the amount of water you will need, but experience will tell you this.

Salt

Salt does not merely affect the taste of your pizza; it is an important ingredient, because it modifies the gluten and this contributes towards the quality of the product. When the dough is rising salt slows down secondary fermentation. This makes the bubbles smaller, and the pizza will keep longer and be crustier. When using strong flour mixes, salt should be added towards the end of kneading, but for weak flour it should be dissolved in water to improve the gluten network. Salt should never come into direct contact with your yeast because it can damage it. Fine salt or sea salt is preferred (which is that we will always refer to) or if you are really constricted to use normal, thicker salt it should be dissolved accurately in water.

Italian recipes often specify the amount of salt as "q.b." which means *quanto basta* or to taste. Some say it only takes 50-60 grams per litre of water, whereas other use as much as 90-100, or anywhere between 2 and 2.5% of the weight of flour. Most pizza makers throw a handful of salt into the mixing bowl, and experience will surely tell you how big a handful needs to be. My handful will certainly not be the same as yours, but as I only ever use mine I know pretty well how much is needed.

Oil

Traditionally, nothing other than extra virgin olive oil must be used. However, this is a fairly expensive ingredient and it has a strong flavour which can overpower many other flavours, so not everyone is agreed on its use. For these reasons, a wide range of oils can be used instead of extra virgin, even if we have given it pride of place in our recipes. It certainly is the best type of oil you can possibly use.

It's used to make your dough elastic, ensuring that the gluten holds, and spreading all the carbon dioxide throughout the dough as it proves. Generally speaking, you will need somewhere between 50 and 60 grams for every litre of water, over 100 if you want a soft crust, up to a maximum of 150 in case of a hard dough.

A drizzle of raw extra virgin on a pizza that's just come out of the oven is heavenly.

Yeast

There are three different types of raising agent, from completely natural yeast or *mater yeast* - very rarely used, but soft and tasty – to completely artificial, which are widely used in food making but not so often in pizza dough. Brewer's yeast either fresh or dried is probably the most widespread version.

Yeast is so important, we have set a special chapter aside for it.

***

Starting with these basic ingredients, here are some of the things pizza makers put in the dough to improve the taste.

Milk: not just milk – some people even use soy milk to make the dough softer. Too much milk turns the dough brown.

Cream: from milk to cream is a very short hop. Fresh whipping cream or its UHT alternative from the supermarket shelves can be mixed with milk or water.

Emulsified lard: lard is used to keep dough soft. I have seen lard used mostly by people making take-away pizzas, because the pizza keeps better when it starts going cold while some others use a specific product. As well as emulsifying, lard also helps keep the flavour and smell of a pizza by cooking it from the inside at high temperatures. The best type to use is white, from the best pork fat, which has not been processed in any way and with no additives. This is used for both round pizzas and slices.

Vegetable oils: either peanut oil or olive oil. Olive oil makes a pizza softer and more fragrant, and peanut oil makes it crunchier. You will need somewhere between 50 and 100 grams per litre of water, but this varies greatly like, for example, in Dante's Mix where there is very little oil because there is some lard instead.

The oil must be added towards the end of kneading, but for poorer-quality flour it should be put in with the water to bind the protein better and make a more homogenous gluten network. Too much oil can slow down proving and over colour the dough.

Butter: as an alternative to oil, butter is best used when you want very soft dough or when making pan pizza. Unlike oil, it makes the dough less elastic, especially when rolling it out, but the taste is very good.

Egg: some people only use the yolk, others only the white, and yet others use the whole egg.

Beer: used because of the golden colour it imparts to the dough, and for its flavour. When used with brewer's yeast it can completely alter the proving. It is like an explosive and needs to be handled with care. For novices beer can really backfire on you!

An old pizza maker used to tell about the time he hadn't made enough dough for what he'd call "a memorable night". By lucky coincidence his pizzeria was taken over by a lot of young people who had just left a concert, and he appetizerd he didn't have enough dough. To not lose money, while he sent some friends off to other pizzerias to get extra mozzarella and other toppings, he went into the work room and started mixing some new dough with beer, to speed up the rising process.

When he was asked why he didn't do that all the time, he said he wanted his customers to like his pizzas for being tasty and easy-to-digest, and this couldn't happen with such a rapid process. Since none of those young concert-goers would ever be back, it wasn't something that bothered him too much...

Sugar and honey: in the same way as salt goes into cakes, a little sugar can be used in pizzas to improve the flavour and to give the final product a lovely golden colour.

Coloured bases: some pizza restaurants, on the look-out for unusual flavours and new ways of presenting the pizza, make the base of their pizzas green, orange, or red by adding spinach, carrots, beetroot, or chilli peppers to change the colour and make their menus more interesting.

Lately, other ingredients have been added to improve overall product quality and make up for any mistakes in the kneading, or simply to alter the flavour. There are companies which aim at improving the effectiveness of the flour, given its importance, either by designing additives or even new flour mixes. The only problem is the infinite range of products.

Renowned is the famous Manitoba wheat, the malt and soy lecithin that should be added in inverse proportion to the strength of the flour (the higher the W, the less you need). You can buy flour with added wheat germ, flour for crusty dough, with natural yeast incorporated, made from durum wheat with bran for an interesting-looking product with a fuller taste, flour for direct or indirect mixes, for short, long, or average proving times, durum flour, ground winter wheat, other cereals such as spelt, barley, or even rice, small amounts of which can be added because they often make the bread-making process more difficult but which are sought after by the growing number of people who love natural products. In particular in recent years, the use of soy flour has increased greatly because it makes the dough much lighter and easier to digest, and hardly affects the flavour. Another ingredient we need to look at is the potato. Many recipes say it is good to add a bit of potato, because it makes the dough softer and a little sweeter. This must be the case, because there are mixes available now with this ingredient added to the flour.

***

The difference between the *basic dough* and one containing one of these added ingredients is very personal and you cannot make prior judgement largely because the final result depends in great measure upon the skill of the pizza chef.

However, it must be stressed that the basic dough made with good-quality ingredients and according to proper procedures is perfect from every point of view.

A pizza cannot be judged as "bad" merely because it is simple, and the use of lots of different ingredients will never cover up a lack of pizza-making skills.

Given the importance of the basic dough this is where we shall begin.

Note: For the sake of simplicity, I'll keep mixing and proving in two separate chapters.

Impasto Base

Basic Dough

1 litre of water

50 grams of salt

1.8 kilos of strong flour milled to 00 finesse (W 260-280 or more)

50 ml of extra-virgin olive oil

fresh brewer's yeast

Place the water into your mixer and mix in the finely-chopped yeast. Pour in half your flour (preferably sieved, as is the case with every type of flour) and mix until you achieve a uniform consistency. Add the remaining flour, with the salt and oil very gradually with the mixer turning and let it mix until the dough is properly mixed and becomes perfectly smooth. Take the dough out of your mixer and lay it on a work surface.

***

This brief explanation allows us to make some important considerations.

1. Units of measurement

The base unit is not the flour, but the *water*, because this is the best way to calculate quantities for a mixing machine and to count the number of pizzas, as we shall see later. In this figure you can calculate the water, or any other liquids you need to amalgamate the flour such as milk, but not oil.

The main reason that flour is no longer the unit of measurement is that it would be very inaccurate: different types of flours absorb different amounts of water, but a litre of water is always a litre. This is why *all my flour measurements are relative*, because they all depend upon your type of flour. Water and flour are variables that depend upon one another: if you keep one fixed, the other has to be changed. But don't worry! If you used to add water until your dough was smooth and homogenous, now you can add flour until your dough is smooth and homogenous. That's all. Nothing ever changes. As long as your dough is always smooth and homogenous.

2. Mixing in ingredients

- It's not random.
- You can add the oil at the start, with the water and flour, or at the end, either just before you take the dough out of the mixer or as you've

finished adding all the flour. It all depends upon the type of flour you use: with weak flours you put it in at the start, and with strong flours you're better putting it in at the end.

- Salt should never come into direct contact with the yeast because it slows it down. You can set some water aside beforehand to dissolve your salt in, or mix it directly with the flour, as is usually the case with strong flour.

3. When will my dough be ready?

There are two things you need to remember.

- *Consistency* or the ratio of water to flour, which is only approximate if you remember.

- The dough must neither stick to your hands nor be as hard as cement. Between these two extremes is a certain degree of freedom which you will discover very quickly. Unlike the amalgam, the consistency does not affect the taste of a pizza except in a very tiny measure. With softer pizza it is better to have a soft consistency, with crispy pizzas, it would be better with a crunchy base. The consistency greatly affects the speed with which you can lay out the pizza. Everyone likes to work with a particular consistency of their own, but leaving this aside for a moment your main problem is that you will only discover the best water/flour ratio when you start mixing your own water with your own flour.

- *Amalgam*: Good dough is something you can see and feel. You can see it because it **comes away from the sides of the mixer** and it looks smooth, swollen, and frothy; it reminded me of whipped cream. Only when it has been mixed properly will it come away from the sides. If you can't see this happening, there is something amiss: either it's not ready, or you have mixed it too much and it has become hard.

- Mixing should take no longer than about twenty minutes from when you put the first ingredients in. You don't need to keep sprinkling flour as you mix the dough until you think you've got the mix about right, because it's true that the flour will be absorbed but the dough won't be mixed properly. The mixer's job is to amalgamates the dough, it does not just mix water and flour. Ask a grandmother the difference and she'll explain that it's the strength and manipulation of the dough that makes the difference. The fact that a machine does this for you simply means your muscles won't tire, it doesn't fundamentally alter the basic importance of kneading.

-     Something you will have to become familiar with is how your mixer works. Different brands knead in different ways. The final result, however, must always be the same. You must have a dough that is soft to the touch without sticking to your hands, and you must be able to poke a hole in it without too much pressure. Pull a piece off and try to pull it out to see how elastic it is. If it breaks it is not elastic enough, and you've probably put in too much flour and not enough liquid, or you've left it in the mixer too long, or there isn't enough oil. If the mix and the kneading/mixing are right, the dough will be elastic and you can handle it easily. If you cut it, the structure will look like the inside of a sponge. Do this once and it is something you will never forget.

Consistency and *amalgam* are two different things: you can have one without the other, but for a good pizza you need both of them together.

*****

To tell the truth, this recipe would be enough to complete the section on dough, all the basic details are there; its reliability, versatility and diffusion make it the cornerstone of all recognised professionals.

To make changes, all you need to do is change the flour, its strength, add a little more or less salt or oil, change the water or prove it in a different way (as we shall see in the next chapter). There are some who say that such a simple recipe guarantees perfection, and that one only needs to select the right ingredients to ensure that the pizza maker will have the best hope of success.

It is hard to disagree with such a statement, but we wanted to give experienced accounts that you can personalize the dough without compromising the quality. Early difficulties may be due to a variety of factors, such as the humidity of the kitchen, the equipment used, the pizza maker's experience, or the quality of the ingredients used – especially the flour. In fact, almost all the pizza makers who have given us recipes say that success will only come if you use the same flour that they use "…'cause if you change flour you get a different pizza". As we can't say the brand name of their flour, we have referred to it as "W".

I don't want to put anyone out, given that this book was created by my experience, so I'll start off with my old recipe, which is obviously one of the best...

Impasto Dante

Dante's Mix

4 litres of water

4 handfuls of salt (60-70 grams per handful)

5 scoops of flour milled to 00 finesse (a scoop weighted approx. 1.5 – 1.7 kilo)

2 scoops of flour milled to 0 finesse

160 millilitres of pure olive oil (40 ml per litre of water)

100 grams of lard (25 grams per litre of water, or only very little more)

4 level teaspoons of sugar (one spoonful per litre)

fresh brewer's yeast

I used to pour the water into the mixer. I would usually make the dough at the same time of day, somewhere about 9 – 9.30 in the morning, and the yeast and the temperature of the water depended upon the time of year. I would use more tepid water in the winter, and cooler in the summer, but we can look at these things later on.

I'd prepare the water and salt, leave it for a couple of minutes, and add the oil and the lumps of lard. After a couple of turns in the mixer, I'd add the yeast after no more than 2- 4 minutes. Then I'd start adding my flour: three scoops of fine and one of coarse, three times and then the flour would be done.

All these operations took no more than 10-12 minutes at the very most, because I saw that if I added all the flour in one go, I could let it mix a bit longer and this meant the various ingredients could amalgamate better. The mix could look hard at first, but the beaters would gradually make it all soft and smooth, and it would start swelling up to become lovely, just as I wanted it. This is a typical effect after the mixing process, where the softness of the dough is developed by good amalgam.

The dough shouldn't stay in the mixer for longer than half an hour overall, but ideally you should take it out after about 20 – 25 minutes, even though a lot depends upon the type of mixer you use. I have always used a forked beater, although many people think the two speed spiral mixer is better. This mixer warms the temperature of the dough by about five degrees, so I didn't use one. If you mix for less than fifteen minutes, the dough won't be kneaded properly: it takes ten to fifteen minutes to mix the proteins, the glutenin and the gliadin which hold everything together.

A few moments before the dough reached perfection, I'd add my sugar and then leave it a couple of minutes: the sugar would make the edges a lovely brown colour. Adding it at this stage means it doesn't interfere with the yeast.

I used flour from my local mill because I knew the people who worked there and how they worked. To improve the half metre pizza (see Chapter 9: Not Just Pizza) I started using flour with a W of 320. I saw that two scoops of the flour milled to 0 finesse absorbed the same amount of water as one and a half of the finer stuff, but didn't really think about it. I would stop the mixer a bit more often to feel the consistency, but when I saw that the dough came away from the sides I knew it was ready. Then I'd take it out and lay it on the worktop.

If you want to change this recipe, remember to keep the ratio of five scoops of 00 to every two of 0 which is quite a good ratio. If you want to change such as I did I recommend eliminating the 0 flour and substituting it with special pizza flour, but don't change the proportions of flour because a larger quantity of 0 does not make a good dough.

A few things that have changed with time: I used to add the salt, oil, and lard before the flour because they contributed to good gluten; with strong flours you really need to add these ingredients afterwards. Also, the recipe I was taught provided the oil residue that I immediately replaced with good extra virgin olive oil with better than good results.

Weight 230 grams, diameter 32 centimetres. We'll talk about these later on.

Impasto Il Periplo
The Periplus Mix

This mix is the great-grandfather of mine. The pizza maker who taught me it had always used it for a softer, more Neapolitan dough, but he said not all his clients liked it. His clients preferred a wider, thinner, crisper base. He changed the recipe by modifying the ratio of oil to lard, because even the tiniest of changes can make enormous differences.

4 litres of water

4 handfuls of fine salt (about 80 grams per handful)

5 scoops of flour milled to 00 finesse

2 scoops of flour milled to 0 finesse

240 grams of lard (60 grams per litre)

160 grams of olive oil (40 grams per litre)

a small handful of sugar (no more than four teaspoons)

fresh brewer's yeast

The method is the same as above. This recipe is the same as the one I was given with ten grams of lard and 30 of oil. I tried to personalize it and changed this to the result above. Remember that olive oil makes for softer dough.

Weight 230 grams, diameter 26 centimetres.

Impasto Belvedere
The Belvedere Mix

This is the mix I asked a pizza maker for, when I heard he could make "proper" Neapolitan pizzas. The milk is something I do wonder about since this ingredient never goes into a Neapolitan pizza, but the results were excellent.

3 litres of water

1 litre of milk

240 grams of salt (60 per litre)

3.2 kilos of W300 flour

2.2 kilos of soy flour

400 grams of semolina (or durum wheat flour)

1.2 kilos of W350 flour

240 grams of extra-virgin olive oil

brewer's yeast

Mix the water with the milk, keeping one litre of this liquid aside, crumble the yeast and start mixing. After a couple of minutes, mix half the flour with salt and oil, and let it beat. Then add the rest of the flour and the other litre of liquid. Let it mix until it reaches the consistency you want, which must be soft to the touch. If you need to, add only W350 flour. There was no reason for this flour mix, but he said it tasted better.

Weight 250 grams, diameter 28 centimetres.

Impasto Diamanti

Diamonds Mix (for Neapolitan pizza)

1 litre of water at room temperature (the so called acqua ferma)

1.8 kilos of naturally proven flour for desserts (W350 or more)

80 grams of top-quality extra virgin olive oil

50 grams of salt

brewer's (or mater) yeast

Put the yeast into the water with the mixer turned on, then add the flour slowly. When you've put in half the flour, mix the salt with the rest of the flour and add it, then the oil, and mix until you reach the right consistency. It seems a much "leaner" dough than the last one, but if you use good ingredients it'll turn out perfect. You can even add a couple of grams more salt, and up to 100 grams per litre of oil. This will make a softer dough. Neapolitan dough is the softest of all, but it needs to prove perfectly. It would be better to use a tiny amount of yeast, and let it prove for at least ten hours, or to leave the dough in a cold room (4° C) for 18 hours. Even better, according to the best Neapolitan tradition, use the mater yeast and leave the dough to prove for 16 – 18 hours.

Impasto Ducale

Duke's Mix

5 litres of water

250 grams of salt

350 grams of olive oil

750 grams of organic rice flour (150 grams per litre)

7 kilos of flour W300

180 – 200 grams of malt (no more than 2% of the flour. If you use rice flour, you can get away with a bit more malt)

fresh brewer's yeast

This pizza maker mixes the dough one day in advance with very little brewer's yeast so it can prove for a long time according to this outline: mix oil and water, add the yeast, and then the flour and salt. Rice flour means the dough is much softer, more delicate, and easier to digest, but only a very small amount can be used because it makes the baking process difficult and the rising slow. It's like we aren't to obey trade rules, rather use internal rhythm as though we are making a more 'natural' dough, and adding malt is a great improvement. He could even use a stronger flour, but this way seems to be one of the best.

Weight 200 grams diameter 34, or weight 220 grams diameter 28. For double pizzas, weight 380 grams, diameter 45 centimetres.

Impasto Il Duomo Bianco
White Cathedral Mix

1 litre of water

65 grams of salt

25 grams of olive oil

40 grams of extra-virgin olive oil

1.7 kilos of soft flour

100 grams of soy lecithin

fresh brewer's yeast

Mix some dough balls from the night before in the water (½ a ball per litre during the summer, and one during the winter, or a bit more). Start the mixer and add the olive oil and the yeast. Let it beat, and add your flour gradually. Then drizzle the extra virgin olive oil in. Soy lecithin is an emulsifier which binds the proteins together and helps the gluten do its work. Using dough balls from the night before means you use less yeast, and people say this makes the pizza easier to digest. When the dough is ready, put it in a cold room and leave it at least twelve hours.

Weight 240 grams, diameter 25 – 26 centimetres.

Impasto Accademia
Academy Mix

3 litres of water

1 litre of sparkling water

5.5 kilos of W 280 flour

400 grams of semolina flour

1.2 kilos of flour with wheat germ

240 grams of extra-virgin olive oil

200 grams of salt

brewer's yeast

Put the natural water into the mixer with the yeast, and let them mix for a few minutes. Add half the flour mixture and let it mix for a few minutes, until it starts to "stick." Pour the sparkling water in, then add the remaining flour, salt, and most of the extra virgin olive oil. If you're using fizzy water, don't uncork it too long before using it; even if it still seems fizzy after a while, it will be noticeably different. When the dough is almost at the right consistency, turn the mixer off and drizzle on the remaining oil and give the dough another couple of spins.

Weight 250 grams, diameter 34 – 35 centimetres.

Impasto La Terrazza sul Golfo

The Terrace on the Gulf Mix

1 litre of water

1.7 kilos of W390 flour

50 grams of salt

70 grams of extra-virgin olive oil

a half teaspoon of malt

fresh brewer's yeast

Mix the yeast and the water, add the flour, and mix for a few minutes. Then add the rest of the flour, mixed with the malt and salt. The pizza maker prefers a softer dough which then matures in a cold room for 18 hours.

Weight 200 grams, diameter 33 centimetres.

Impasti Scientifici
Scientific Dough

This is the name I have given to two recipes because they're designed for people who want the most technical solution to all their problems where human foibles can't ruin things. It is no accident that some flour manufacturers showed me them, and they are for their products. However, they involve procedures which we have not yet seen.

***

Recipe 1.

2 litres of water at a temperature of 38 degrees centigrade

2.3 kilos of strong flour milled to 00 finesse (W280 or stronger)

1.4 kilos of soy flour

100 grams of extra-virgin olive oil

120 grams of salt

dry yeast: five grams in the winter and three in the summer

Everything begins by measuring the flour with a special thermometer, because we need to consider the rapport between the external temperature and above all that of the water in relation to the temperature of the flour.

Mix the dry yeast in 100 grams of water until there is a little froth on top. Put two litres of water and the yeast into your mixer and give the machine five turns. Then add two kilos of finely mixed flour. After about two minutes, you will have a very liquid dough: add 600 grams of flour, salt, and oil, and give another five turns of your mixer. Then add the remaining flour and drizzle oil onto it from above. The dough will be ready when it stops sticking to the side of the machine, never more than 15 – 20 minutes of mixing time. Let the dough rest on your work surface.

***

Here is another recipe for pan pizza, which uses the same *factor 54* (see Chapter 5).

4 litres of water

7 kilos of flour for pan pizza

200 grams of sea salt

270 grams of extra-virgin olive oil

dry yeast

Put half the flour into your mixer and half the water and let it beat for three minutes. Add 500 grams of water containing the yeast and one kilo of flour, and beat for a further four minutes. Add the salt and 500 grams of flour, and then alternate the remaining flour and the oil, and give it another five minutes to improve the air quality inside the dough. You can make the mixer go a bit faster if your mixer has this option, or let it beat for an extra minute. Remove the dough and put it in a plastic container to rest for half an hour in summer, or an hour in the winter.

If you like you can reduce the quantity of one flour and merge it with reinforced flour.

***

I am sure you have begun to notice two completely different approaches to pizza making: one is meticulous and precise, and is probably more widespread in large-scale production, the precise amount of an ingredient is considered a vital element in the process; the other one is a bit more "homely" and the skill of the pizza maker is much more important. You can see this in the last two recipes, where the pizza maker is a workman who weighs out precise quantities of ingredients, controls the mixing, whereas all the other recipes depend upon experience.

Whatever route you decide upon, remember there are disadvantages too.

A more skill-based system requires a longer training period, and more experience and ability (which you'll never lose), but these are things you can't pick up in a hurry. If you're ill or you can't mix your dough for some other reason, who will take your place? On the other hand, if you have the exact details for a system that someone else can take on, there's always the danger that they'll nick it.

Speaking for myself, I prefer the more skill-based approach where experience is more important than any machine. Actually, this is the hardest thing to learn about the job. How can someone know what to do, when they start off knowing absolutely nothing? They have to learn. It is knowledge gained day after day, learning from mistakes, and only practice and global awareness of the work can offer assurance. I hope my words are clear enough and can help you when it seems tough at the start. If you persevere I know you'll make it through this difficult bit.

Ricetta Anna

Anna's Recipe

This is a recipe my mother gave me, and I think it's the best for pan pizza.

2 litres of water

3.5 kilos of W 320 flour

160 grams of salt

400 grams of extra-virgin olive oil

100 grams of fresh brewer's yeast

As with all recipes, this one can be changed to suit your own personal needs. I substituted the water with UHT milk to have a richer flavour for small, individual pizzas, soft and thick like the Neapolitan pizza, even though water makes it lighter. There is one major fault with this type of dough: milk and lots of oil can colour the pizza a lot, especially when there is a lot of work. I only ever used this recipe for take-aways and when I could prepare things ahead of time.

I used a W 320 flour for long proving times, and did two mixes a week which I'd keep in the cold room. The weight I used was 160 grams, and a diameter of 18 centimetres. The quantity of oil may be a little excessive but if you use a wood-fired oven and allow another proving phase (I'll tell you how in chapter 9), you'll have a pizza that's easy to digest and has a taste that absolutely everyone will love. Even if I used strong flour, I did all the usual things and dissolved the salt in the milk, then added the oil and yeast, and the flour at the end.

Impasto della domenica
Sunday Dough

We have already said that consistency has hardly any effect on the taste of the pizza, but it makes working the dough and laying it out much, much speedier. Saying that everything else is the same, the thing about Sundays is that you need to work ten times faster than on other days to make enough pizzas for everyone. A lot of pizza makers tend to do a lighter dough for Sundays so it is quicker to roll out. The Sunday dough, as it will be called here, refers not to the specific day but to these often frenetic working conditions. It will simply use a little less flour. There's no great difference, because the dough still needs to be elastic and not sticky, compact and properly amalgamated, only the consistency will be a little softer. The difference is barely perceptible, just a few less grams of flour and it'll take you a bit of experience to get right.

This is not some law that you have to obey. It's only a trick which is spoken of behind the counter.

***

Let's have a look at the **golden rules** for a perfect dough.

- The first rule is in choosing you raw materials, which must all be top quality.

- Never mix your dough for more than 25 – 30 minutes, or even better within 20 minutes.

- Whatever recipe you decide on, and whatever method you use, your dough must have the perfect consistency, so it becomes easy to use, and must be perfectly amalgamated. When the dough stops sticking to the side of the bowl, you're onto a winner.

- A good dough must be proved for the right time.

PROBLEMS

There are different types of drawbacks, and the solution for them depends upon the cause. Let us start with those that are immediately visible.

There are two of these: the dough is too hard or too soft.

If you realize this when the dough is still in the mixer, it isn't so terrible. If it's too soft, add some more flour. However, if it's already perfectly amalgamated and it's just a little too soft, you'll have to try harder next time. Speaking for myself, I'd cut it into balls and sprinkle some flour on them. This won't do much, because when you roll them out you'll need more flour anyway and they may stick on your worktop. If the dough is too hard because you've used too much flour, adding more water won't do very much. Try adding a tiny (and I mean TINY) amount of milk, but remember not to exaggerate with your mixing time.

If you only realize when you take your dough out of the mixer, the first thing to do is to promise that next time you'll notice earlier!

If it's too soft, sprinkle some flour on the dough balls, but if it's too hard you'll have to try to understand whether you've used too much flour or left the dough in the mixer too long. Whatever you do, leave it to rest under a slightly damper cloth, then decide whether you should leave it close to the oven to help the rising, because harder dough doesn't prove so easily.

It is a common mistake to leave it in the mixer too long, while you're trying to do a thousand other jobs. When I first started out I thought the mixer worked miracles.

There is no job that is as important as kneading the dough: you'd be far, far better "wasting time" by looking closely at your dough and studying how tiny doses of ingredients can change the magic mix. If you choose one recipe rather than another, don't think you'll have to occupy your time searching for difficult to find ingredients, because it won't be enough throwing them all into the mixer and switching it on. If any starred chef and I were to boil two eggs, theirs would surely come out better, even if they let me do the one the hen had just laid. Why is obvious; they know how to make it stand out and you have to learn this too. Look at your dough carefully and see how it changes, the chemical, physical and mechanical properties will improve each ingredient. Out of all the rules this is the most important.

RESTING AND WEIGHTING

When the dough is ready, it is usually cut into balls, each of which will become an individual pizza, and then left to prove.

Before this, it has to **rest** a little. This is not vital, but is usually for the better.

Leave that big lump of dough in a damp cotton cloth for 15 – 30 minutes, even if some say you can leave it for an hour or two. The purpose of this operation is to make the dough more elastic to roll it out. Resting will not affect the quality or taste of the dough, but simply makes working it easier.

I'm sure you've noticed how the dough in a pizzeria keeps its pizza shape once it has been rolled out, whereas it "shrinks" when you try the same thing at home. This is because the dough is not placed under a damp cloth. Remember: don't use any softener in the washing machine because lavender pizza is not so good!

I liked to use an almost dry cloth so the consistency wouldn't change, but it's not a great problem in any case. For example, if you notice that your dough is too hard, use a damper cloth; if it's too soft, wring the cloth out as much as you can. Resting can take place with the dough in a covered plastic bowl, which stops it going hard on the outside, and then leaving it for anything between half an hour and one hour.

Some pizza makers refer to Resting as the first proving phase.

***

After the dough has rested, or immediately after the mix if you don't let it rest, you're ready to make balls of a certain **weight**. There are machines that can do this for you, but they'll never be as good as an experienced pizza maker. The heat from your hands and the pressure you apply will make for a much better dough. You won't believe me when I tell you what a simple hand movement can do for the final flavour of a pizza. I didn't realize it at first, but handling the dough made it much more crispy and crumbly. Try it yourself with two balls of dough: one well handled and one done carelessly, then make two pizzas and taste the difference. You'll realize how important this stage really is.

Amateur pizza makers don't know, but professionals are well aware that the taste of pizza is also determined by the *ratio between the diameter and the weight* of the ball, so these factors are extremely important.

You can decide to make a pizza any weight or size you want, but it must always be the same weight and size. If there is a difference of 10 grams or 1 cm you won't be able to tell the difference, 20 grams or 2 cm you will note, 30 grams or 3 cm is too much, and it'll be a different pizza. Try it and you'll understand. With the same dough, make some different balls of the same weight but roll them out to different sizes. Taste the pizzas you make in this way, and then always use the best ratio.

There are some "standard" sizes such as 24-26-28 centimetres (Neapolitan), 30-32-33 centimetres (Pulled or Stretched), and 45 centimetres (Giant, Super,

His & Hers, Family, and so on), all corresponding with the blades you use to put them into the oven. For guidance, a Neapolitan pizza and a pulled one need the same amount of dough, about 200 grams, but you can always experiment. For example, if you make a 32-centimetre pizza with a ball weighing 220 grams, it will taste different from a 35-centimetre one using the same amount of dough. If you're happy with that size of pizza but you want to use more dough, you can use 230 – 240 grams or even more, according to what you or your customers want. Usually a giant pizza will need something like 400 grams of dough (twice the normal amount, more or less), whereas a pan pizza might need up to 600 grams.

Let's now look at weighing. Use a good set of scales to get the right amount per ball of dough, and then roll it into a sphere.

You block the ball with your hand, holding it still and turn it onto the marble worktop. There is no sense in making it turn like a spinning top if you don't use the right tension, and you don't roll it properly. The balls must be compact and firm, and there shouldn't be a hole underneath. An old pizza maker used to say that to be really perfect the dough balls must be egg-shaped, and if your movements are right the dough will take on this form.

Make sure they are all perfectly formed, that underneath they are closed, and they don't lose shape when laid out on the tray. If you push them lightly with a finger, the imprint should disappear almost immediately.

Weighing shouldn't take too long because the dough has already started proving and it can become difficult if you take too long. Sometimes the dough can become tough because your kitchen is too cold and the yeast has "caught a chill" as we say. This will cause the dough to be hard and difficult to pull, there is the possibility of being flat because it may not rise properly since the yeast hasn't been allowed to do its job. Put the dough somewhere near the oven so the yeast can do what it's supposed to.

As you weigh the balls of dough, lay them in the drawers so that the first ones are going to become the first pizzas you make, and the last ones the last. Cover all the drawers, especially the first one; if you don't, the dough will form a crust which will affect the aesthetics of the pizza, but not taste. Sometimes it can be hard to make balls of dough because it is lumpy: this means you've mixed it very badly. Don't try putting it back into the mixer for another blast.

***

When making **pan pizza**, after mixing the dough you can decide if you want it to rest under a damp cloth or in a plastic bag. When weighing, the same idea is used but the actual weight is different according to the size of the tray you are going to use. Balls of dough may be oval or spherical, depending on how you want to use them. To tell the truth they don't even need to be closed as perfectly as the stretched pizza, simply they can be handled and given the form before being put to rise.

Here are some number for you to consider: anarchy is the general rule here...

400 grams of dough for a 35-cm tin, and 20-25 minutes in the oven

500 grams of dough for a 35-cm tin, and 25 minutes in the oven

500 grams of dough for a 28-cm tin, and 30 minutes in the oven

For a rectangular tray measuring 60 x 40 centimetres, use a 1.5 kilo lump

There are those who put the dough directly into the tray to prove after resting, which cuts out a whole stage.

Tips from the Pizza Chef

-     If you forget to cover the first tray, lay a damp cloth directly on the dough balls to dampen the crust. Unfortunately, it won't go away completely.

-     Keep a damp cloth handy so you can close the dough balls more easily: the water makes it stick better. Remember to wipe the work surface when you've finished.

-     As soon as you put the dough aside to rest, clean the mixer immediately. If it hardens on the bowl, it'll be a devil to get it off afterwards.

-     If you find your mixer is too small, don't rush off to buy a new one: think about mixing two different doughs, maybe one you can put away in the cold room for a couple of days.

Dough and Numbers

The weight of dough balls crosses the amount of water.

One litre of water is the same as fifteen dough balls of 220 – 230 grams or one drawer, and two litres is the same as two drawers or thirty pizzas. If you need eighty pizzas a day, or 100 or 200, you can easily work out how much dough you'll need to make. This is an almost perfect system, because a couple of dough balls too many or too few won't mean the end of the world. But that isn't all. If you use this system, you can work out how many pizzas you've made at the end of the evening by seeing how many dough balls are left. That way you can get a fair idea of the money you're earning.

Obviously, if you make pizzas using a different weight of dough your figures will have to be adjusted. Work them out for yourself, and that way you won't be left with too much unused dough when cashing up at the end of the evening, or having to turn customers away because you've run out. All the time you spend in trying recipes and working out figures will be more than paid back by making your work easier and quicker, and will turn you into a proper profession

APPENDIX

Those which you will find below are not the complete regulations relating to *Good Manufacturing Rules*, but a simplified version.

PERSONAL HYGIENE

The pizza maker and all those who work in the restaurant are a showcase. Do it in a way that will be a good business card.

Check that they always have a clean uniform and headgear.

They need uniforms and shoes to use exclusively in the workplace to prevent the transport of microorganisms from outside to inside the kitchen and they need to repair eventual wounds, cuts or burns with protective and waterproof dressings to be replaced often.

Seeing that we work with our hands, they must always be clean. It's best not to wear rings, bracelets and watches during work that can collect dust and carry dangerous germs close to our product.

Hands have to always be washed:

- Before starting work: before preparing the dough and removing it from the machine, turning the balls, observe the rising...
- After handling raw products: bringing sacks of flour into the laboratory, checking the package of prosciutto, the tomato tins, the mozzarella...
- After going to the toilet.
- After touching any kind of rubbish, but also the wood.
- After each work interruption e.g. the postman arrived.

HYGIENE IN THE WORK ENVIRONMENT AND THE EQUIPMENT

Food must be protected from eventual microorganisms present in the air with the use of lids, plastic wrap or other ideal means. Keep the sacks of flour on suitable hoppers and those opened for consumption in a closed cabinet and protected from dust. Do not sweep or lift dust during the processing of foods.

Keep the workplace free of pets, insects, mice, cockroaches, ants. There are commercially suitable "traps for crawling insects" that you can buy in any supermarket. Use them and replace them often: they are practical, fast, economical and secure.

Like your hands, the equipment should always be kept tidy and well cleaned.

Work surfaces, counters, tables, cutting boards, tableware, plates, trays, the oven and mixer must not contaminate the food. Buy them made from easily disinfected material to facilitate the work. Keep the refrigerators and cold rooms always clean, but above all check that the temperature of food storage is adequate to ensure you don't leave the goods to perish.

FOOD HYGIENE

Purchase primary materials only from approved suppliers and avoid the products that don't undergo the necessary checks: in the unlikely event that they give you problems, how can you say it's not your fault but that of the person who sold them to you?

Check that your confections are sound, suitable and duly labelled, the arrival temperature of food such as frozen foods, mozzarella, eggs... and the expiry date of products in stock.

Avoid contact between raw and cooked foods and between foods of different origin such as meat and vegetables, cold meats and cheese e.g. don't put the meat near the seafood. If you already have toppings ready for use, put them in special containers that you recognise immediately. You'll be faster.

Keep perishable foods like milk, meat, cheese, food semi-prepared with an egg base at temperatures between 0 ° and 4 ° C. Keep frozen food at temperatures below -18°C. Thaw frozen food in the fridge and use them in the day. Leave food at room temperature for the shortest time possible before use. And remember that preparations that require cooking are the safest.

Always maintain hygienic behaviour throughout all the work.

Once internalized these simple precautions will give you less waste of primary materials, a more pleasant restaurant, and the quality of your product will be safer, all things that your customers will surely appreciate.